WHAT'S UP WITH WATER?

HOW CAN WE SAVE WATER?

by Karen Latchana Kenney

Consultant: Marla Conn, Reading Specialist, Read-Ability

BEARPORT PUBLISHING

Minneapolis, Minnesota

Teaching Tips

Before Reading

- Look at the cover of the book. Discuss the picture and the title.
- Ask readers to brainstorm a list of what they already know about saving water. What can they expect to see in this book?
- Go on a picture walk, looking through the pictures to discuss vocabulary and make predictions about the text.

During Reading

- Read for purpose. Encourage readers to think about water, its role in life on Earth, and why we need to save it.
- Ask readers to look for the details of the story. What are the reasons we need to save water and the ways we can?
- If readers encounter an unknown word, ask them to look at the sounds in the word. Then, ask them to look at the rest of the page. Are there any clues to help them understand?

After Reading

- Encourage readers to pick a buddy and reread the book together.
- Ask readers to name three ways from this book that we can save water. Go back and find the pages that tell about these things.
- Ask readers to write and draw a picture of something that they learned about saving water.

Credits:
Cover, © Potapov Alexander/Shutterstock; Title page, © Chepko Danil Vitalevich/Shutterstock; 3, © Yuri Samsonov/Shutterstock; 5, © Bartosz Hadyniak/iStock; 6, © hanhanpeggy/iStock; 7, © Denis Burdin/Shutterstock; 8-9, © topseller/Shutterstock; 10, © CK Foto/Shutterstock; 11, © MNStudio/Shutterstock; 12, © Moyo Studio/iStock; 13, © Zyn Chakrapong/Shutterstock; 14, © nicolas_/Getty Images; 15, © robert_s/Shutterstock; 16, © YinYang/iStock; 17, © schulzie/iStock; 18–19, © SolStock/iStock; 20, © borgogniels/iStock; 22, © pupahava/Shutterstock, © MicroOne/Shutterstock, © ideyweb/Shutterstock, © BlueRingMedia/Shutterstock; 23BL, © Willowpix/iStock; 23BM, © FatCamera/iStock; 23BR, © Santiparp Wattanaporn/Shutterstock; 23TL, © Konmac/Shutterstock; 23TR, © yoh4nn/iStock

Library of Congress Cataloging-in-Publication Data

Names: Kenney, Karen Latchana, author.
Title: How can we save water? / by Karen Latchana Kenney.
Description: Bearcub books edition. | Minneapolis, Minnesota : Bearport
Publishing Company, [2021] | Series: What's up with water? | Includes
bibliographical references and index.
Identifiers: LCCN 2020039085 (print) | LCCN 2020039086 (ebook) | ISBN
9781647474911 (library binding) | ISBN 9781647474966 (paperback) | ISBN
9781647475017 (ebook)
Subjects: LCSH: Water conservation—Juvenile literature.
Classification: LCC TD495 .K46 2021 (print) | LCC TD495 (ebook) | DDC
333.91/16—dc23
LC record available at https://lccn.loc.gov/2020039085
LC ebook record available at https://lccn.loc.gov/2020039086

For more information, write to Bearport Publishing, 5357 Penn Avenue South, Minneapolis, MN 55419.

Printed in the United States of America.

Contents

We Need Water 4

Saving Rain. 22

Glossary 23

Index 24

Read More 24

Learn More Online. 24

About the Author 24

We Need Water

People drink water to stay **healthy**.

We use it to wash our bodies.

Everyone needs clean water.

Is there enough?

Our Earth is covered with water.

But ocean water is too salty to use.

Some of Earth's water is still ice.

We can't drink ice or wash with it!

We get water from lakes and rivers.

Do not waste water.

We have to be smart when we use it.

Let's look at how we use water every day.

How can we save water?

Only use the water you need.

Turn off the tap when you brush your teeth.

Keep it off when you rub soap on your hands.

Drip, drip, drip!

Oh, no!

The water is on and no one is around.

Be sure to turn off the tap when you are done.

Water **garden** plants well!

Let the rain water your plants.

Save rain in a **barrel** for when it is dry.

Sometimes our lakes and rivers get dirty.

Then we can't use them.

We need to take care of our water.

Keep **litter** off the beach.

We can all save water every day!

Find ways to use less water.

Do your part to keep water clean.

Each small bit helps.

Saving Rain

Save rain to use in your garden. Here is how a rain barrel works.

Glossary

barrel a large bucket to hold things

garden an area where plants are grown

gutter a tube along the edges of a roof used to catch and move rain

healthy well and not ill

litter things that have been thrown on the ground

Index

clean 4, 21
garden 16, 22
litter 18
ocean 6
plants 16
rain 16, 22
tap 12, 15, 22
water barrel 16, 22

Read More

Boone, Mary. *Conserve It! (Saving Our Planet).* North Mankato, MN: Capstone, 2020.

Boothroyd, Jennifer. *Be Water–Wise, Super Grover! (Go Green with Sesame Street).* Minneapolis: Lerner Publications, 2020.

Learn More Online

1. Go to **www.factsurfer.com**
2. Enter "**Save Water**" into the search box.
3. Click on the cover of this book to see a list of websites.

About the Author

Karen Latchana Kenney writes and edits books about water, nature, and famous scientists. She lives in Minnesota with her husband and son.